Contents

Introduction

Checking 'Em Out and Sizing 'Em Up is one of a series of books. The complete set is called **Ready-Set-Grow!**

Checking 'Em Out and Sizing 'Em Up deals with opinions, prejudice, and discrimination and can be used by itself or as a part of a program that utilizes all of the **Ready-Set-Grow!** books.

Checking 'Em Out and Sizing 'Em Up is specifically designed so that children can either read the book themselves or have it read to them. This can be done at home, church, or school. When reading to children, it is not necessary to complete the book at one sitting. Concern should be given to the attention span of the individual child and his or her comprehension of the subject matter.

Checking 'Em Out and Sizing 'Em Up is designed to involve the child in the concepts that are being taught. This is done by simply and carefully explaining each concept and then asking questions that invite a response from the child. It is hoped that by answering the questions the child will personalize the concept and, thus, integrate it into his or her thinking.

Everyone has opinions, from the time he or she is very young. Our opinions affect the way we feel about ourselves and the world around us, and how we act. For this reason, it is important to help children understand that what they believe to be true may simply be their opinion and that differing opinions may exist.

Checking 'Em Out and Sizing 'Em Up teaches children, through examples, the different kinds of opinions that people might hold on a single issue. It shows that people can change their opinions and that opinions affect the way people act.

Checking 'Em Out and Sizing 'Em Up carefully explains for children how their thinking is influenced by the places, situations, and people they have contact with as well as what they read, hear on the radio, and see on television. Although these influences are powerful, children can have control over their own opinions, and the book outlines six steps they can take in forming their opinions. This process is extremely important, as the book explains, because a person who pre-judges an issue before thinking it through carefully is prejudiced. Being prejudiced is unfair and often leads to discrimination.

Checking 'Em Out and Sizing 'Em Up is designed to help children form their own opinions with integrity and keep their minds open to the possibility of changing their opinions. Children who grow up with this ability will be better equipped to live healthy, prejudice-free lives.

Checking 'Em Out and Sizing 'Em Up

You are a human being, and because you are . . .

you have many opinions about many things.

You began having opinions when you were very young . . .

and you will continue to have opinions for the rest of your life.

What is an opinion?

Do you know?

The first chapter of this book will answer this question for you.

Chapter 1

What Is an Opinion?

To help you understand what an opinion is, answer the following questions:

What do you think about two children fighting?

What do you think about a park that is run-down, cluttered, and filled with broken equipment?

What do you think about children using guns, knives, poison, or matches?

Your answers to these questions are your opinions.

An opinion is what a person thinks about something.

The thing a person has an opinion about is called an "issue."

Every opinion is either . . .

> for,
> against,
> neither for nor against, or
> undecided.

An opinion that is _for_ is an opinion that is in agreement with the issue.

Gloria thinks that girls should be allowed to play baseball.
Her opinion is <u>for</u> girls playing baseball.

An opinion that is <u>against</u> is an opinion that is in disagreement with the issue.

John, Gary, and Todd think that the girls should not be allowed to play baseball. Their opinion is <u>against</u> the girls playing baseball.

An opinion that is <u>neither for nor against</u> is an opinion that does not agree or disagree with the issue.

Richard does not care whether or not the girls are allowed to play baseball. His opinion is <u>neither for nor against</u> the girls playing baseball.

An opinion that is <u>undecided</u> is an opinion that has not been decided.

The teacher doesn't know whether or not the girls should be allowed to play baseball.

The ISSUE being thought about and decided upon is:

Should the girls be allowed to play baseball?

The OPINIONS are:

Gloria, Barbara, and Chrissie have an opinion FOR.
John, Gary, and Todd have an opinion AGAINST.
Richard has an opinion that is NEITHER FOR NOR AGAINST.
The teacher has an opinion that is UNDECIDED.

What is your opinion about the issue. Should the girls be allowed to play baseball?

Are you . . .

        FOR_____

        AGAINST_____

        NEITHER FOR NOR AGAINST_____

        UNDECIDED_____

Whether the opinion you have right now is for, against, or undecided, one of the most important things for you to know about it is that an <u>opinion can change.</u>

When an opinion changes, it can become either stronger or weaker, or it can change completely into a new opinion!

What do you think happened to the opinions of these people?

A second important thing for you to know is the way your opinions affect the way you act. In other words, what you think about something will affect what you do.

For example, when John's opinion was <u>against</u> girls playing baseball, he did not play baseball with the girls.

But when John's opinion changed and he was <u>for</u> girls playing baseball, he played baseball with them.

So, remember two important things about your opinions:

1.   Whatever your opinions are right now, they can change.

2.   Your opinions affect the way you act.

You already have many opinions about many things.

Where did your opinions come from?

Do you know?

The next chapter will anwer this question for you.